Cow-Head Goddess

Mia Hoffman

BookLeaf Publishing

Presentation by *BookLeaf Publishing*

Web: www.bookleafpub.com

E-mail: info@bookleafpub.com

ISBN: 9789395756273

First edition 2022

DEDICATION

This book is dedicated to the kid tapping a tablet in the backseat, trying desperately to rhyme with "North Dakota."

ACKNOWLEDGEMENT

Special thanks to Brennan, my best friend, critic, and competition,

and Mither, who gave me loose-leaf and love.

Projection

Two girls lie in a dual constellation
still, on the charred carpet
drifting in a dismal place
(where they are ignored.)

One strand of hair reaches for the other
jet black and crimson,
both with the ambition to stifle the opposing,
settling into a wary truce
to be clotted with colored wax
(found hours later.)

A silver cord is attached to their navels,
anchoring them to this plane.
On the other end,
their souls bobs expectantly
waiting for release.
(they were told of it by witches.)

Jet Black feels her insides shift,
parting to let the electricity through,
the sense of crowning and scrambling,
something serpentine, thrashing to breathe
(a soul is like a botfly.)

the galaxy swirls with tendrils

of cheap incense. dragon's blood and something
else
sweet, chemical, meant to escape out the
bathroom window,
but has leaked into the ether, turned the stars
yellow.

Crimson clamors under the bed for a new
candle,
vanilla, goodness and innocence
(this is her torch.)

Jet Black has lost her serpent to the disturbance.
(I got so close.)
Crimson lets the match burn down her fingers.
(me too.)

Prodigal

Home appears to me
in a failure of language,
a postcard of a faceless structure–
the march of windows goes unmistaken for eyes,
any candidate for a mouth disfigured into
entrances.
I follow the logic of the shape
to draw the rectangle and roof,
but there is no humanity to the memory.
It is only a place.
It can not even grieve.

So I go to the lily, who lived there first,
protecting the window in which
a child and woman had prayed,
asking the moon for advice.
She tells me the room has been coated eggplant,
and there are no artifacts within it.
It is neutralized now as if
there were never a catalyst,
no elaboration of a soul.

I go to the mirrors, who do not react.
They report dispassionately
I am bones and angles,

and speak vaguely of a soft governess
with blonde hair.
They consider aching,
but think better.

I lower into the bathtub,
an illicit venue,
and find femininity
still hidden in the stopper.
The water doesn't remark at all,
that was its strength.

Braid

My hope is that
ourselves in photographs
prove that we can touch,
that we remain a landscape,
it is not too late.

My fear is such
when you become
an empty leather armchair,
I will still sit before it
for a braid.

Objectivity

Progress is marked by
hairpin legs. Modern touches, plastic ferns. If
signs go unlaminated, if
the desktop is licked clean of stain, and the
clients are called Honey,
you have undone your legitimacy,
you have made yourself an attic nurse.
the way of Professional is to
create fortunes for the suffering & send them
off,
to grow your nails long, and speak of death as
a Long Weekend.

an administrative oracle
anointed us, aliases with which to greet
Pain (from across the room,
taking care that the wound

does not pool round our shoes.)

Grass

You
and I
stand in the
blanched grass
eyes fixed
on
one blade
until we
tear
smearing
the other
into
old
barrack
colors

the sun
tells
indian time
our faces
cave in
were there
always
so

few
joys?

I grow
lilies
You won't
look at &
You grow
children
to keep
inside
& we too become
bristles

I'm
sure if
the wind
died
one of
us
would speak

but why?
the
grass
does

Inertia

I say to no one I am too sad to write, to entice
A crib from a hospital couch, a wool facade on
bloated rubber
warmed by downy fibers & drowned beetles.

The blue dark may crawl beside me
to listen for
a deepening of breath.

Moonlight frays the curtains
speaking imperfectly in my ear
of dreams and hemispheres—

I am young in the north,
chewing the day,
fussing with the part of my hair.

in the south is a cannery
where mothers trap their lives
for greater use.

Rez

If I make it back there,
I worry it will not be wild. I think of
the betrayal of a paved road,
the subterfuge of funding,
the phantom hands of Franklin still
fussing and fumbling.

They put makeup on the water tower, replaced
fading letters in the signs,
scrubbed thirty years of anguish from
the flanks of tunnel slides.
did they cut the prairie weeds, and line the walks
with perennials?
did they splinter all the crosses of the highway
memorials?

I was a barefoot child with fond callouses of
poverty, and now
grown, I loathe to walk the plains of suburban
commodity–
but what does a mutt know of social progress,
authenticity?
There is less quantum in my veins than has been
shed for prosperity.

Pacifico

The blue is permeating,
we are breathless in its wake.
I am a drunk, baptized in the Pacific,
spitting seaglass on the page.

We have adored but not this,
amniotic and profuse,
Twenty-odd and losing
without defeat.
We have laughed but never like this,
christened by wind,
gospel with the roar of the sea.

There is talk of tattoos.
A mile walk
reachable by the striations
of a palm. A band, a song
A fruit.

I decide
distantly, with rosy assurance
these are the polaroids
I will touch
as an old woman.

Thief

Somewhere between
merlot and curry I said plainly
I felt no responsibility to your fear,
spilling my glass into yours
as if the wine forgot the evening.

Somehow on miles of sidelong glances
and the moon resting its chin on the road,
a measured instinct to ransom kindness
reached for the radio,
wound my jaw,
just to leave you searching.

Someday
maddened by the softness of your faith,
I will shame you so that
you turn out my pockets, and know what I took.

Consumption

How ill-fated, to be
impaled with insistent appetites
and sent stumbling,
clutching our stomachs.
We consume, as insects do,
but have eaten that which competes,
for we were given pointed teeth.

The world has been rendered.
In the colony is heard
a song to savor the ice,
so wonderfully cold on the tongue!
and to candy any rind downed
in Eden for our young.

How doomed to be this organism,
to sit at a table
and return to dust.
We must feast beneath frescos
to remember death,
and hope to stay full enough.

Church

It began as all failures do,
from the cabal of a body

a treacherous Inspiration
wafting from the Id,
demanding truth, which (it knew) existed
beneath the circles
of damning flesh

to strain to Become
for the reward of Being,
that was the nature of faith.

So was surrendered
my hearth to suffocate,
a garden to discipline,
And erected a cathedral of bone.
I prayed until
the sanguine taste
exhausted flavor.

Host

The feat is to say
come and sit in my chair
without the sting of irritation
kneeling as though it were
an honor,
to sweep crumbs as if to make a home
for the stranger.

The modus is to hold tight to a gaze,
and settle your features into
an empathetic drip
which stews confessions.

To host another's fragility
is to harbor the sadism
which wears an apron,
and cuts cake.

Unlife

The muse pulled so neatly from death,
as applique from film,
to comfort the polite assertion
all are torn from their business,
and are forever set upon usefulness,
howling, sentimental–
as a continuation.

A body is contented, sitting in its flesh,
enduring the little sufferings, the sicknesses,
to luxuriate in the certainty
feeling one's mortality
is the singular attraction.

A ghost is the sweetness of a corpse,
A delightful extraction.

Talon

You were sleeping in the living room, flanked
by my taste, and withered
beneath a throw blanket long since
needing to be washed

I was adjusting to the dimness
moving through the dark like music
with a plastic hairbrush in the
hand which plans and strikes. I thought about
mauling you, barraging you in blows
to give back the hurt you loaned

but my body is cold in the middle
as I forage for my rage. I know it's
in there somewhere, thirty minutes ago
my cries scared me, and my hand
froze in a talon

I thought about suffocating you,
how you would fight and flail,
your mind blanched and panicked with pain
like mine

but I turn,
back to the room

and the manufactured peace

Dawn

What is in the window beyond is
of little consequence.
There are progressions in your face
more distinctive than the dawn
peering over my shoulder.

You are explaining yourself
first deliberately,
then, with the momentum of being alive
and unknown,
the talk becomes kaleidoscopic
as your past animates.

Facets of minutiae I will never remember,
fragments which allude to a greater story
that your heart deems I have heard.
This is vital,
forgetting your manners–
describing the colors, assuming–
trusting–
I will see each hue.

What is in the window is a sunrise
which requires no coaxing,
a light which does not brighten

as I dedicate attention.
It is poor competition.

Teen

There will always be more to love,
The world is lousy with it.
There is little to do in the kind of crisis which
cries
in the mirror and folds itself over a dam.
The gift of the descent of the sinking feeling
is to keep it company,
to sit freckled with rain in your first car
and let a piano from before you were born
explain the art of hurting.

Optimism

This place rots like a back molar
God forgot he had.
For the next apocalypse
I'll be better dressed, he
already paid the band.

Cow-Head Goddess

Spread thick on a chaise, the Cow-Head
Goddess
(Ah, you again)
reviews the time-lapse
I have arranged for her verdict;
a flickering composite of years spent
Coiled and recoiled on the carpet, too empty, too
full
Sitting resolute dents into the washing machine,
appearing in the mirror like an omen.
A long exposure, staring through the car
windshield until
a blush of absurdity moves us to promise–
like children–
we are done crying,
and ready to go in.

Cow-Head Goddess is at the projector now,
having disturbed an obsolete shelf,
and threads a ribbon of film. Deaf to protest.
I see I am eighteen, and new. I am bent at a table
Chronicling the punctures of a sewing needle
which you trail down my neck.
In the way I loved you, from the very first, the
ink

stains compromise, assured and consummate,
only the first hieroglyph of flesh.
Cow-Head language. Your sigil.
The pain was how I understood it as permanent.

The footage jumps and crackles,
We are reading together under a young tree,
then near a brown river,
then aloud, in an unnameable accent, as you
hold the wheel with one hand,
saving the other for me.

I have no patience for this sentimentality,
The deceptively simple, the sepia. I stand,
Casting a silhouette across a montage,
whereupon
we are aging through art museums,
coming to rest at contemporary, the precipice of
our twenties,
confronted with Picasso in Barcelona.
I watch as I cross the gallery to you–
standing before a 1905 portrait, moved to tears
by proximity–
and envelop you.
That was only June.

"It's not all here," I say.
"Where is the misery?"

The Cow-Head Goddess motions.
(At the end.)

25